HELP, MY MONEY KEEPS RUNNING AWAY!

HELP, MY MONEY KEEPS RUNNING AWAY!

Dr. Larry D. Brown, Sr.

iUniverse, Inc.
New York   Bloomington

HELP, MY MONEY KEEPS RUNNING AWAY!

iUniverse books may be ordered through booksellers or by contacting:

iUniverse
1663 Liberty Drive
Bloomington, IN 47403
www.iuniverse.com
1-800-Authors (1-800-288-4677)

Because of the dynamic nature of the Internet, any Web addresses or links contained in this book may have changed since publication and may no longer be valid. The views expressed in this work are solely those of the author and do not necessarily reflect the views of the publisher, and the publisher hereby disclaims any responsibility for them.

ISBN: 978-0-595-43807-5 (pbk)
ISBN: 978-0-595-88136-9 (ebk)

Printed in the United States of America

iUniverse rev. date: 11/10/08

This book is dedicated to the memory of my mother, Mary Irene Brown who passed away in June 2000, and my father, who at the time of this writing is eighty years old.

CONTENTS

Introduction

This book was written to show the average man or woman how to increase his or her net worth by dealing with one's self. "Help, My Money Keeps Running Away" is a "must read". You will find the positive strength within yourself to overcome the most depressing of situations. I am not concerned with your background-whether you have a college degree, high school diploma, a GED or DEC (don't even care). The important thing is not what's around you, but what's in you. You need to point to yourself and say, "Greater is He that is in me than he that is in the world". Whether you are single, married, separated, divorced or just don't know what you are-this book can help you. There are so many problems that can be traced back to money. Low self-image, worry, illness, stress, and the death of dreams are a few of many of these catastrophic results. This book is designed to help identify the hindrances in one's life and eliminate and rectify them in order to produce more positive results. Now let's clear the air right now, I do not claim or pretend to be some financial guru or genius. I am an average American like most of you reading this book. I happen to be a Black American. I have a Bachelor of Science degree in Business, a Master of Divinity degree, an earned Doctor of Ministry degree, and pastor a church. All of my degrees cost money and time (as I did not obtain them through a mail order). Aside from pastoring for over twenty years,

I have been buying and selling real estate as well as owning my own businesses for more than twenty years. I have saved money in jars, socks and even shoe boxes. I have invested in stocks and bonds for many years. I have been to many seminars-from Carlton Sheets to Donald Trump-and am currently a member of the Donald Trump Institute. OK, enough with the small talk because your money may be running away as you read this, so lets see if we can put our heads together and stop that money from running away.

CHAPTER 1

▼

LET'S BE REAL

Let's be real, I need money and so do you. If you don't need or want any money, on your next payday please send me your paycheck! Don't cash it; just sign the back of it. My address is on the back of this book. If you are going to be helped by reading this book, you are going to have to be honest, not with me, but with yourself. Nothing will change and nothing will happen until you, (that's right I'm talking to YOU) take the first step. And that is the REAL DEAL. I have not taken my valuable time, researched information and shared my personal experiences only for you to simply read my book. No, sir. I did all this to help you make a change in your financial life.

There are a lot of people that you and I know, people we care for deeply, who, if their thinking concerning money doesn't change, will be in for a lifetime of struggle and problems. The Bible refers to this as a generational curse. In others words, when each generation seems to do the same or worse then the previous generation-a perpetual erosion exists. Somehow a generation of people has been birthed that does not have the drive down in their souls that their fore-parents had that caused them to seek a better way of life when all the odds were against them.

You see, there's a certain amount of education that even the schools do not and can not give. I remember my school years and how the teachers taught me Math, English, History, Science, Spelling and even, Physical Education, but throughout kindergarten to the twelfth grade, no one taught me about money and how to save and invest it. No teacher said to me, "Larry, remember never spend all your money" or "Boy, buy yourself some shares of stock as soon as you graduate and hold on to them so in twenty years you'll be rich". Where was that "great teacher" in my school days, and yours, whose quest was to pull out the best in us? Everyone's situation is different, but I can tell where my mentor was. I guess (as it should have been) my greatest teacher in the art of finances was my father. He never gave me direct advice concerning money while I was a child. But in all my years of growing up in a family of seven children, I can not remember one time, not one, when money was needed and my dad did not provide. It was only after growing up and becoming a man, (you see there are some that are grown in age but their actions say they are still children) that I began to understand why my father worked more than one job. In this day and time it is called being an entrepreneur. You see, my father worked a nine-to-five job for someone else, but when he got off, he went to work for himself. If you are not making enough money on your job, what law says that you have to only work one job? I know this upsets some people, but if you want more money, you've got to make more money.

My first experience working for my Dad was at the local recreation center picking up trash. Later I was promoted to cutting the grass. I remember my father telling me not to cut the grass around the swing set while the little white children were playing. Today I'm still picking up trash and cutting grass, only now it's at my home or one of my rental properties, or one of the office buildings that I own. "Thanks, Dad, for teaching me what the schools did not". As I look back now, I realize that in reality my father was actually teaching me.

You see many times black children will learn more from what we show them then they will from what we tell them. My dad taught me a great lesson about pride during those days at the recreation center. You may be saying, "What does that have to do with my money running away?" It has more to do with it than you may think. If you are not willing to deal with where you are right now, you may as well stop reading. Yes, we were cutting grass and picking up trash, but dad was making money and teaching his children to become thinkers and entrepreneurs at the same time. The point is this-if you do not take pride in yourself and deal with where you are right now, and if you just hate your job and every one on it, you are more likely to continue to be a spender and not a saver. Thus, you help your money to run out of your hands and into the hands of someone else. Now, I'm not trying to make you mad, but again, let's be real. The fact is no one will make you spend every dime you make and guess what, NO ONE WILL MAKE YOU SAVE ONE DIME EITHER.

CHAPTER 2

▼

LOOK BEFORE YOU LEAP

There are many ways to waste resources and bring poverty upon oneself. We have already mentioned one-incurring debt. When you incur debt, a sizable proportion of your money goes for interest and carrying charges. You end up paying more and receiving less. Another irresponsible use of resources is indulging in impulsive buying. You see something and you want it, so you buy it. You haven't checked the quality of the product. You haven't compared prices. You haven't determined what other costs may be involved in keeping and using the item. You just spend on impulse.

You cannot misuse your spouse and expect him or her to stay with you. You can't misuse your car and expect it to run smoothly. You can't abuse your friends and expect them to always be there. The same applies to your money. You cannot misuse money and expect it to stay with you. Many people are impulsive buyers. A working definition of an impulsive buyer is simply "A person who buys things without thinking". Now, I'm not against a person having nice things, but a nice pair of tennis shoes doesn't have to cost two hundred dollars. Your money is not in any hurry to leave, so why are you spending it so quickly? If you are going to keep your money and manage it properly, you don't ask where the money went; you tell it where to go. I do not believe that God wants his people to be in debt. Scripture tells us, "The borrower is servant to the leader" (Prov. 22:7). Any time we incur debt we assume a servant relationship to our creditor because we must now work for him to pay our debt. God tells us not to become a servant to any man, but instead to serve Christ (1 Cor. 7:21-23).

There are two kinds of debt, good debt and bad debt. So, which one do you have? Buying a house or land is good debt. Buying five hundred dollar rims is bad debt. Get the message? God knew the type of pressure that debt could put on us, and He did not want us to be involved in it. So His Word says, "Owe no man anything" (Rom.13:8). He makes one exception-our debt of love. That's the only debt we are to constantly pay.

Be leery of get-rich-quick schemes. Boy let me tell you, no, I better not. Well, let me just say this; I've been tricked before by get rich schemes-from surfing the internet, to sending money to companies promising to turn my one hundred dollars into five hundred dollars in just five days, which they did. The only problem was the business disappeared in four days and my money was gone.

The Scripture says, "He that hasteth to be rich hath an evil eye, and considereth not that poverty shall come upon him" (Prov. 28:22). So often we hear of grand schemes: Invest five hundred dollars in this and in three weeks you're going to have one thousand dollars profit. Two weeks later you'll have two thousand dollars more profit, and in another month, four thousand dollars profit. A couple of months after that you can take a vacation to the Bahamas. You'll have earned thousands of dollars by that time. You think, "Wow, here's my opportunity, and opportunity knocks only once. I've got to invest in this". You have a garage sale and sell everything that's not nailed down. You sell your wife's ring, borrow all you can from her folks, and go zipping on back with the money. You really are into this thing only to arrive at a very costly conclusion. You join and then you get three to join and then they get three people to join ... Listen folks, been there, done that and I got a tee shirt. It's called help my money keeps running away! The Bible says, "Discretion shall preserve thee, understanding shall keep thee" (Prov. 2:11). You need to be very discreet and knowledgeable about money-making schemes. We also read twice in Proverbs that in a "multitude of counselors there is safety" (11:14; 24:6). If someone comes to you with a business opportunity, you don't necessarily say "no". "Yes" could be the right answer, but get some sound financial counsel.

CHAPTER 3

▼

WHAT THE SCHOOLS FORGOT TO TEACH US

When considering the financial mis-education of African Americans, we should not forget the contributions of the public school system. One would think that surely the public school system would teach African American children (and all other children) how to manage their money. This, however, is not the case. The primary job of the public school system has been and continues to be, to teach children the basic needs to enter America's work force. Apparently, those who govern our public school system do not consider money management a basic requirement for entering the work force.

Therefore, a paradox has developed whereby African American children are taught the American dream but are not taught how to secure that dream. This dilemma has occurred because few public schools teach students the role the American dollar plays in securing the dream. Schools also fail to teach a systematic approach for building financial security. Public schools do a good job teaching children about independence, but a poor job teaching them about investing. They do a good job teaching children about the principles of American freedom, but a poor job of teaching them about the principles of the American free enterprise system.

The tragedy of this paradox is the confusion it creates in the minds of African American children who graduate from public schools without the financial skills they need to compete successfully. Many African American high school graduates have no idea of the financial responsibilities they will face in life; therefore, many are forced into the job market armed only with a false sense of financial reality and a distorted expectation of living the American dream.

Consequently, the public schools, the churches, and the civil rights organizations have each contributed to teaching African Americans that all men are created equal but have failed to teach the importance of creating wealth. Thus, each of these institutions has contributed to the financial mis-education (or the lack of financial education) of African Americans.

This lack of financial information has kept many from enjoying the American dream. Many African American families have learned to cope with experiencing the American nightmare instead. For many families, poverty has become a normal way of life. Scraping pennies has become a habit; maintaining the status quo is easier than trying to break out of the cycle of poverty. We are living in a society where 49% of black families do not have a father in the house and are living below the poverty level. Now brothers don't get mad at me, but as long as the system keeps you thinking that making babies and not being there for them is cool, then the money that should be in that home is steadily running away. Consequently many of these families unconsciously leave their heirs a legacy rooted in poverty, which is passed on from generation to generation.

Nevertheless, there is good news for the millions of African Americans who represent the poor, working poor, and nearly working poor. The good news is that you can still enjoy the fruits of the American dream once the art of using financial resources effectively has been discovered. What I have done in the past-and continue to do even now-is to read and study what successful people read and do. Sounds so simple doesn't it? But many see no importance in knowing what others have done or are doing. If you are serious about keeping your money from running away, read books and magazines on what rich people invest and how they invest it. I know you are not Bill Gates and can't buy a million shares of stocks at one time, but what about ten shares of the same stock he buys. Many wealthy people share where they invest in publications such as books and magazines. You may not be able to soar with the eagles right now, but who's stopping you from learning where they got their wings. One thing I have learned over the years is, whether I like it or not, I must read. I have been the pastor of a local church now for over twenty years; however, one must read more than just the Bible in order to keep money from running away. I find myself reading as much as possible on money and finance in order to discover ways and ideas on keeping my money where it should be-with me. In other words, if the schools don't teach it and the preachers don't preach it, that means it's up to you and me to teach ourselves the art of keeping more money than we spend.

CHAPTER 4

▼

YOU'RE NOT WORTH A DIME

We cannot over estimate the importance of increasing the net worth of African American families. Every dollar invested by African Americans increases the wealth gap that exists between black and white Americans. This by-product of net worth-building holds enormous implications for the economic future of African Americans.

Many believe that earning a decent income is all that is required to win the game of financial success. This rationale undermines the importance of saving and increasing your net worth over time. Let's briefly review the economic advantage of increasing your net worth.

On the eve of the Civil War, records indicate that more that fifty percent of free blacks were paupers; all free blacks collectively held less than one-half of one percent of the nation's wealth. In the 1960s more than fifty percent of all blacks were still impoverished and barely held one percent of the nation's wealth. Not much has changed since that time. The latest census indicates that African American per capita net worth is $10,651 compared to $51,191 for white Americans. African American efforts to achieve income parity with their white counterparts have done little to decrease the wealth gap that exists between them. It is time for us to focus more attention on the importance of net worth-building to achieve income parity with white America.

The ownership of more net worth-building assets will greatly improve the economic fortunes of the African American community. For we will not just be saving money, we will be investing in stocks, homes and businesses. Furthermore, while individual African American households are increasing their personal net worth, they will simultaneously increase the collective economic power of African Americans across the nation.

More African Americans can also achieve their financial goals if they concentrate on systematically increasing their net worth. Now understand this, your net worth is not based on how many cars you have or suits you wear. Net worth is simply taking the value of all of your assets and subtracting the total of all your liabilities from the total assets. I am sorry to inform you; your car is not an asset-nor is the gold around your neck. If you are spending more money on cars, jewelry, and clothes than you are saving, then you are forcing your money to run away. I am not against enjoying material things, but come on now, love yourself enough to put something in the cookie jar for your future. Look, if you have less money in the bank then the cost of tennis shoes on your child's feet, you've got a problem. If you start saving a little at a time, you will begin to experience a difference within yourself. There is a sense of self love that flows when you love yourself enough to put some money aside for you. You may not be able to save a thousand dollars a month, but come on now-what about ten, twenty or even a hundred dollars? Please, not for God's sake but for your sake, stop spending every dime you make because if you don't, you really won't be worth a dime. It's ok to put a few dollars in a jar or sock, but in order for net worth to exist, your money must grow. I suggest that you check out banks and ask questions about checking accounts that pay interest. You see, two percent isn't much but it's still better than zero percent. Also, many on-line banks give great interest rates. At the time of this writing, E-Trade offers a savings account paying five percent with no minimal balance. Check it out. The bottom line is that I'm trying to convince you to start where you are and save something. You see there's no need for me to talk to you about investing in stocks, bonds or real estate if don't even have a saving or checking account. Let's play a game. Close your eyes and picture an old man or woman sitting in a chair, his or her steps have grown shallow, eyes are dim, hair is gray, back is aching and children are gone. That's you ten, twenty, thirty, forty or fifty years from now. Please love that older person you saw enough to give him or her some money today, that he or she will thank you for tomorrow. Trust me.

CHAPTER 5

▼

STOP LOSING YOUR COOL

It is time to STOP getting mad at everybody else for your choices. (So don't get mad at the bill collectors for calling, they are just doing their job). What I'm saying is STOP GETTING MAD AT EVERYONE ELSE FOR YOUR CHOICES. Ok, so you made some bad decisions in the past-so have I and everyone else reading this book. What I am suggesting is that you don't let your past destroy your future. Get mad at yourself and do something positive about it. There are over four hundred billion cells in our brain. Let's use them to think of ways to better ourselves and stop that money from running away. You see, it does not take a lot of energy or time to blame the world, parents, spouses, employers, "the white man" and now the Mexican for our money woes. But it does take time and energy if we refocus and take the responsibility for ourselves in order to stop our money from running away.

If you want your money to stop running away, try being grateful for what you have. Look, at some point you must begin to believe in yourself and deal with the fact that there are no more free lunches. Understand neither your past nor the present is your future. If you are so angry and mad at the world that you can't work for minimum wage, and choose instead to stay unemployed, you are already defeated. Your thinking has to change. Now don't judge me too quickly. My first job (outside of working for my father) was shining shoes at the airport. My next job was at McDonald's cooking hamburgers. I was thankful then and I'm thankful now. I practice regularly thanking my money for coming and staying with me. When I buy stocks, bonds or just make a deposit, I tell my money that I'm sending you away to go and get some of your cousins and bring them back to live with me. Doesn't make sense does it? But, my friend, this is what is called the law of attraction which states-what we focus on the most the universe will bring to us. If you constantly say, "I'm broke", "I ain't got no money", or, "I can't pay my bills".

Guess what-the law of attraction states that the universe must give you what you ask or focus on the most. The Scriptures say it this way, "As a man thinketh in his heart, so is he". Declare with me right now, "My money is not running away, my money loves to be with me and when it leave my hands it's only to go and bring back some of its friends and cousins".

CHAPTER 6

▼

KEEP THE FAITH

The religious faith of African Americans and their success are seen throughout history. We pray for everything. If there is something we want badly enough, we will pray for it. We pray for houses, new clothes, and even good fortune at the casino. In almost every African American community, business, and organization-on almost any given day-you can hear, "*God's will be done*", "*It's in God's hands now*", or "*In God we trust*". What I find interesting is that in spite of all of this praying, many African Americans haven't realized how to maximize the spirit of success. Several reasons appear to account for this situation. Many see God as a "super being" living in the sky ready to punish or reward them depending on their actions. Many still believe that a poor life is a Christ-like life.

Many view their relationship with God as interpersonal and not personal. In other words, a relationship that is inside of them and limited, rather that a part of all that they are and all that they do. Many see God as a being to depend on instead of a God that empowers. Many believe that in this world we must suffer and be rewarded for suffering in the next world. These notions about God undermine the ability of some African Americans to understand and enhance their spiritual capital.

Many successful African Americans, such as Oprah Winfrey, Bill Cosby, Dr. Benjamin Carson, Terry Williams, Susan Taylor and many others understand and readily use their spiritual capital. Most have a calming presence about them. At first, this calmness may appear as confidence, but there is something unique about the way they talk, walk, and act-a demeanor that announces to the world, "I realize and reverence the existence of an all-powerful God."

There is a law of success that states "Our internal reference point is our own spirit, and not the objects of our experience". When you are in touch with your spiritual self, you will not let outside situations, circumstances, people, or things keep you from enjoying your highest good or economic potential. I am certain that you have heard the old expression "Problem Child", and perhaps someone said it about you growing up. You do not have any money problem that is so great that it cannot be overcome. Whatever else happens, keep this one fact in mind, for every problem there is a solution. You see, there is the law of opposites: for every night there is a day, for every valley there is a mountain, for every problem there is a solution. Whatever you do, don't ever, ever give up. Just remember you have the power to believe, "I have the strength to face all conditions by the power that Christ gives me" (Phil. 4:13, NLT).

Understand this, you, like many people, have money problems. I congratulate you first of all because only dead people don't have problems. If you have problems that means you are alive. One of the neat things that God has been teaching me is that in every perplexing problem there is a striking opportunity. Your money problems are great opportunities for you to learn, to advance, and to overcome-not only for your own good but also for your family's well-being, and for the glory of God.

We must come to learn how to develop the right attitude toward money, how to practice sound Biblical principles of finance, and how to sow the seeds of faith and thereby receive a multiplied return of unlimited supply. I'm ready for mine, how about you?

A professor of psychology at California State University claims that 90 percent of all illnesses are caused by money worries. A recent women's magazine featured a survey which showed that 75 percent of all worries are about money. You know it and I know it. We don't need a survey to tell us that an overwhelming majority of all our worries are either directly or indirectly related to money problems. You have a good mind and are an intelligent person, so why, I ask you, should you worry and fret over money?

You need to be mindful of this very important fact, worrying over money will not change anything. It will not add one day to your life. It will not pay one bill. It will not solve any financial dilemmas. It will not make you any happier, but instead will make you quite miserable. So I ask you again, why should you worry and fret over money? Have faith in God and in yourself to believe that you are going to make more money, keep more money, and the money that has run away from home is on its way back and bringing some friends with it.(If I were at church I would say, "Can I get a witness!").

CHAPTER 7

▼

TAKING CONTROL

When I was growing as a child, my mother and father had the responsibility of instructing me where I could and could not go (Thank God I listened MOST of the time). As my children grew up I took on the same responsibility as my parents did for me. After I grew up however, I had to take control of my own future and destiny. In other words, I had to start making intelligent decisions concerning my life. What you must realize concerning money is that until you take control of your money, it will always do and go exactly where it wants to go. With God on your side, you can and will take control of your money.

Decide now that you will *never worry about anything that is not in your power to change.* Choose to live one day at a time. Refuse to carry problems and anxieties from one day into the next. When a day is over, drop the curtain. Put it in God's hands. You can't do anything to alter that day. That day is done. Reach forth to the new day realizing today is the first day of the rest of your life. Because we know God's mercies are new every morning, stop worrying about the future. Who holds the future? God does. I belong to a God who is in charge of the future.

So many would have us think of religion as some far off pie-in-the sky so to speak. Well, I want to tell you that God is concerned about the bread for your physical needs here and now. I believe that God is interested in the energy crisis, and He cares about the inflation that eats away at all of our incomes. He is intensely interested in you and your financial situation-your dreams, aspirations, and goals.

I don't care who you are or how old you are. I don't care if you live up town or down town. The bottom line is this-no one is going to manage your money for you. And dear friends, unless you make up your minds to become responsible for managing your money, you are going to continue to be in a mess financially. It does not matter how spiritual you are or how often you attend church; you have got to get a grip (and a strong one at that) on your money. If not, guess what? You're right. It's going to keep on running away to live with someone else.

If you are passionate about solving your money problems, (and I believe you are) then take one giant step forward by deciding that, come what may, you are going to manage your money. I didn't say your spouse's or your children's money. I said yours. You cannot make your husband, wife, or children (over 18) do anything. It is our job as good stewards to tell them what should be. What God puts directly into your hands becomes your responsibility. To fail to decide to manage your money, as far as I'm concerned, is a sin and a curse.

In Luke 19, Jesus shares the familiar parable about a wealthy man who has great holdings and enormous assets. Preparing to be gone for a period of time, he divides his assets among several of his servants to manage and care for in his absence. Upon his return, he calls in the servants and asks for a full account of how well they have done in managing what he has given them. One has excelled in his management and another has done quite well, but the third has completely failed to take the responsibility of being a good steward. The point that Jesus is making is this: Each of us is given the responsibility of something to manage. The fact is that it is not how much we have been given that counts, but rather how well we manage what we have. Be faithful over a few things in order to gain many. "But it is always true that those who have, get more, and those who have little, soon lose even that" (Luke 19:26, NLT).

I believe it is Biblically and psychologically correct that a man should carry the bulk of the financial responsibilities (Please don't tell my wife I said this!). A Real man will spend time thinking about his financial problems and seeking solutions to them. For every problem there is a solution. Often a man's lack of aggressive leadership in the area of finances creates a vacuum of worry and stress within his wife. A woman's greatest need is for security. Happy is the wife and blessed is the husband who through his financial leadership provides an atmosphere of security. I do realize that some homes do not have a strong male figure and still more have no male figure at all. Often times due to separation, divorce, death, or because some strong sister chooses to remain single, women become the sole provider. To these I say, God looks at our situations and circumstances and equips us, if we are willing to be equipped, with what we need to not only run this race, but also finish it. Ask yourself these questions: Do you want to keep on struggling to make ends meet for the rest of your life? Would you like to get on top of things financially? What is it that you want to achieve financially in your lifetime? In the next five years, what do you want to accomplish with your money? Do you have any financial plans for the next 12 months? How about the next five, ten, or twenty years?

Multitudes of people are sinking financially simply because they have no financial blueprint. Would you contract with a builder who was known for not using blueprints to build a new home? If you would, it would be like throwing your money away. You are a whole lot smarter than that! And yet, many of us keep throwing our money away simply because we have no pattern or plan by which we manage our money.

Someone once said, "When you fail to plan, you are planning to fail." There is no area of life in which this is more true than in the area of finances. To plan is to predetermine your course of action. The only alternative to planning is to act without forethought. Instead of leaving your financial future to chance, it is far better to decide now where you want to go and to start planning how you are going to get there. Decide where it is you want to go, and plan how you are going to arrive at your destination. If you tell me, "Let's go to California next week", my question is "How are we going to get there?" Are we going to fly, drive, take a bus, or a train? In other words, there must me a plan. Take an honest look at where you are financially. Come on now. No one is around and no one knows what you're thinking (except God and he's trying to help you). What's in your savings and checking accounts (If you don't have one get one)? What assets do you have (sorry a car is not an asset if you're making payments)? How much money do you have in your shoe book or pillowcase? Do you have stocks, bonds, mutual funds, or real estate? Do you own your home? Are you renting? Are you still living in your crib with mom and dad?

Now I will tell you exactly how to get a financial blue print for yourself. Now don't be afraid because the enemy builds upon our fear. To start seeing your financial blueprint, get a copy of your credit report from all three major credit bureaus. Everyone is entitled to at least one free credit report a year. If you have not received one in the last twelve months you can go to annualcreditreport.com to receive a free report from all three agencies. There are other web sites that claim to offer free reports, but if they ask for your credit card number, IT'S NOT FREE. The credit reporting agencies are below for your reference.

Experian	Trans Union	Equifax
P.O. Box 9701	P.O. Box 2000	P.O. Box 105167
Allen, TX 75013	Chester, PA 19022-2000	Atlanta, GA 30348
1-800-509-8495	1-800-916-8800	1-800-685-1111

I know you may feel like many others who don't want to deal with their credit. But it's a step in the right direction to becoming successful and causing your run-away money to come back home. You see, my friend, your credit report tells others with the money-such as banks, mortgage companies, etc. whether or not you are trust-worthy. Don't stop reading now because you've come to far to turn back now. Credit reports give institutions your payment history-whether you have paid and are paying your bills on time or not. This area alone has caused many good people to allow the enemy to fool them into thinking that this is just how they are. You ought to give the devil a black eye and get your credit repaired. If you have had bad credit ever since you were a teenager, and that's been over twenty years ago, something is very wrong. Unless you have a lot of cash lying around, you are going to need credit. Ok, your credit is so bad that you can't even borrow a quarter to make a phone call. Don't be dismayed; there is still hope. "So where do I start?", you may ask. Right where you are. I told you at the beginning of this book-"Let's be real".

What is Credit?

Simply defined, credit is financial responsibility. For lenders, this is interpreted as your ability to borrow money for products or services, with the guarantee (and assurance) that you will pay for them at a later time. As you know, credit enables us to purchase our homes and auto-mobiles more easily. In fact, without credit, very few people would be able to pay full price for these items at the time of purchase. Can you imagine trying to come up with one hundred thousand dollars in cash to pay for a home? Would you even be able to "scrape together" an extra fifteen thousand dollars for a new economy car? Not many people could. It's just not realistic. And it's a fact of life. Through credit, however, most people are able to buy these types of items. There are so many people who will never be helped in their financial situation, not because they cannot learn how to help themselves, but because they continue to play the game of avoiding financial realities. The longer people play this game, and the older they get, the sadder it is.

If you are fortunate to have good credit, one thing you should be mindful of is not being too anxious to share your good fortune with others. When others come to you with the offer of co-signing on a loan with them, don't feel bad about declining their offer. I know you may feel compelled to help, but many relationships have been damaged and even destroyed because of unpaid loans. I could probably pay my mortgage for an entire year if I was to receive all the money that I have loaned that has not been repaid. At least six different times the book of Proverbs warns us about loaning money to unreliable people (Prov. 20:16, for example). Whoever you loan money to, whether a friend at the time or not, one thing is sure-if he doesn't pay you back, he won't be your friend in the days to come. There is a subtle temptation to allow debts to friends to slip by unpaid. Resist that temptation. "It is poor judgment to co-sign another's note, to become responsible for his debts" (Prov. 17:18, NLT). Unless you have the extra cash on hand, don't co-sign a note. Why risk everything you own? They'll even take your bed (Prov. 11:15). Now, there are times when co-signing is done between business partners. That's a good plan provided that they each have good credit.

Remember the only way to climb a mountain is one step at a time. The truth of the matter is there are people we meet and greet daily whose credit report says they're wearing a mask and under that mask is a person who either pays bills late or doesn't pay at all. You see, the better your credit report, the greater chance you have at borrowing and investing in things such as homes, land, and investment property. There are many books written on how to repair bad credit, I encourage you to get some good books on the subject and start repairing your credit today.

CHAPTER 8

▼

LAZY MAN

A lazy man will not be rich. You must avoid the pitfall of laziness.

It appears that whenever there is laziness, it is sooner or later followed by poverty and financial bondage. When there is no desire for gainful employment, one of the most loving things we can do to help motivate the individual who lacks motivation is to remind him that the Bible says "If any would not work, neither should he eat" (2 Thes. 3:10). (I hope this wasn't for you).

CHAPTER 9

▼

GOD WANTS YOU TO PROSPER

God wants nothing but His best for you. It is God's intention for His children to reap the riches of His marvelous creation. Out of the treasure chest of the Bible comes this divine wish for you, "Beloved, I wish above all things that thou may prosper and be in health, even as thy soul prospereth" (3 John 2). There is no special blessing in being poor. Obviously a person cannot be very happy if he is existing in poverty.

God is not blessed or glorified, nor is his name honored, when he sees his creation living on less than the best. Poverty is never God's will for anyone. You are a child of the king, and a king is not glorified if he sees his son, the prince, going without the things he needs. If Jesus Christ were standing beside you this moment, I am quite sure he would not praise poverty. Instead he would proclaim, "My father is rich in houses and land; He holds the wealth of the world in his hands. What my father has is yours." Prosperity is your God-given heritage. Having money is your God-given heritage. But whatever is good and perfect comes to us from God, the Creator of all light, and he shines forever without change or shadow" (Jas. 1: 17, NLT).

So stop playing yourself cheap and stop letting people play you cheap. Have you ever noticed that broke folk are the only ones that keep telling you they don't need any money? Don't forget the law of attraction. Look, understand this; there is no limit of supply with God. There is no aspect more crucial in the quest for money than this one: *Who is your source?* If your employer is your source, you are going to be disappointed. If your attention is on things you can't afford to buy, you are in for double trouble. If you are trusting in your own intelligence to gain more money, then you are in for some depressing days ahead. If you are looking to another person to supply your needs, you are going to go without. But if you look to God, He will neither disappoint you nor let you down. Put God first. Make God your source, and you will succeed in solving the financial problems in your life. I am a firm believer in Biblical instruction. In everything you do, put God first, and he will direct you and crown your efforts with success. Do you want financial success? Then put God first in all your money decisions. Do you want the finer things in life? Then give God your best. It is not *what* your source is, but *who* your source is that will make the difference. Every time I take my eyes off Jesus and start to rely on what I think are my own capabilities, or those of another, to supply my needs, it doesn't happen. But when I look to Jesus as my Lord and Provider, He faithfully provides an increase and abundance every time. If my money seems to be on a running away spree, I go to the source. Believe the promise: "But my God shall supply all your needs according to his riches in glory by Christ Jesus" (Phil 4:19). If you are not receiving an abundance of good things in your life, chances are this is because in some way you are limiting God. It is the most natural thing in the world for the abundant supply of good things to flow from God into your life. It is His desire for you.

Even if you are on a small or limited income, don't feel unworthy, because God is your source as well. Some have not yet learned the secret of unlimited supply. Have you heard the story of the jumping flea? There were at least 10,000 fleas spread like a blanket across the teacher's desk. To entertain themselves they started playing a rather wild game called The Jumping Game. Higher and higher they jumped, again and again, trying to out jump all the other fleas. Then it happened, the kill-joy teacher sneaked up on them and covered them with a jar. Not knowing what had happened, they kept hitting their heads on the top of the jar as they jumped up and down. But after being battered on the head a few times, they got the message and stopped jumping so high. After that they would still jump, but would stop an inch from the top of the jar. After an hour the teacher removed the jar, but those fleas never knew the difference. In their minds, they had fixed an imaginary ceiling. Although the jar was removed, they refused ever again to try to jump any higher than the self-imposed ceiling that they had set in their minds. I want to let you in on a very important secret. I call this the secret of unlimited supply. You must be careful not to cut off the flow of supply that God wants to give you by thinking like a victim. Who put the cover over your jar and stopped you from jumping? Really I couldn't care less. What's important is the fact that it's ok with God to have money. Let you and I declare right now, "My money is going to stop running away from me today!" Now say it again like you mean it. The Bible says this about a man: "If he plants the good things of the Spirit, he will reap the everlasting life which the Holy Spirit gives him".

One of the most potent things in nature is one of the tiniest-the seed. Within every seed there lie explosive possibilities. One little seed planted in the earth can bring forth enough food to feed many people.

In the spiritual world there is nothing more powerful than faith. Jesus spoke of this unmatched power when He said, "Verily I say unto you, if ye have faith as a grain of mustard seed, ye shall say unto this mountain, remove hence to yonder place; and it shall remove; and nothing shall be impossible unto you" (Matt. 17:20). When you put seed and faith together, you join the most powerful of both natural and supernatural forces to provide you with unlimited supply. Whatever seed you give in faith, God Himself will multiply back to you many fold.

I'm going to tell you something that makes no logical sense. An accountant would throw up his hands and say this is horrible teaching. It just doesn't add up at the end of the pencil, but here it is anyway. I believe with all my heart that when a person is in financial difficulty, the very first step to getting out from under depressing debts is to put God first by tithing. You see, tithing is *not a debt you owe but a seed you sow.* It is a seed that unlocks the door to greater supply in your life. The Scriptures teach us this very significant lesson. While the children of Israel tithed to the Lord they prospered, but whenever they withheld the tithe from the Lord, hardships came upon them. God said, "Bring the whole tithe into the storehouse, that there may be food in my house". Test me in this and see if I will not throw open the floodgates of heaven and pour out so much blessing that you will not have room enough for it" (Mal. 3:10). We will discuss the blessing of tithing in the next chapter, as we continue God's way to prosperity.

CHAPTER 10

THE BIG TEN

Another preventive action to employ to keep your money from running away is tithing. To get God's best you have to give Him your best. Don't kid yourself, you can't give God leftovers and fool him into thinking you are giving him your best. There is no bigger fool than he who keeps fooling himself. You do want God's very best and highest in life, don't you? Proverbs 3:6, 9-11 instructs, "In everything you do, put God first, and He will direct you and crown your efforts with success. Honor the Lord by giving him the first part of all your income and he will fill your barns with wheat and barley and overflow your wine vats with the finest wines."

It has been my observation while working with hundreds of people over the years, that those who never learn to practice the principle of tithing are forever having a multitude of money problems. On the other hand, tithing alone does not guarantee financial success, but it is the most important step to take concerning your money. As you tithe you can rely, not only on God's help in your financial life, but also on His bountiful blessings. The Bible says, "A sensible man watches for problems ahead and prepares to meet them. The simpleton never looks, and suffers the consequences" (Prov. 27:12, NLT). In the passage of time you can reasonably expect some unforeseen financial emergencies. Sooner or later the roof is going to leak, or the tires on the car are going to wear out, or the car is going to need a major overhaul. So be wise, look ahead, and plan for the unseen and inevitable. "The wise man looks ahead. The fool attempts to fool himself and won't face facts" (Prov. 14:8, NLT). It pays to plan ahead.

The only way to plan for future expenses is by saving. I learned the art of saving by becoming a tither-giving God ten percent and living off ninety percent. Then I began giving God 10 percent, saving 10 percent and living off eighty percent. I'm trying to tell you if you do it God's way, you can't go wrong. "The wise man saves for the future, but the foolish man spends whatever he gets" (Prov. 21:20, NLT). However, many people say, "I can't even pay my bills as it is! How do you expect me to do so if I have to give the Lord ten percent off the top?" It is not for us to understand. You need only to "Trust in the Lord with all your heart. Never rely on what you think you know. Remember the Lord in everything you do, and he will show you the right way" (Prov. 3:5-6). People who tithe report that an intangible "something" happens to their finances. They find they are not wasting money as they used to do. They don't make bad financial decisions. As they walk in obedience to the Lord, they find many blessings. I am reminded of a man who once said, "I wanted to buy a new car because the transmission was going out on my old one. I was severely tempted to stop tithing so I could make my car payments. As soon as I made the decision to continue tithing, I discovered a mechanic who said the original analysis was wrong, and the car could be fixed for three dollars."

What more do we need than God's assurance to take Him at His word and to trust Him? Why don't you give it a try? You will be pleased with the results. The Bible has many other instructions on how to go about giving our tithes and offerings to God, in order that He remains first in our lives. Some people measure their amount of giving by how much they can reduce their income taxes at the end of the year. So they give very little all year long, but if it looks like they've had a good year and a sizeable gift to the church will be a badly needed tax deduction, they will give. But this kind of giving negates the blessings of God. Such once-a-year-giving is also a violation of Scripture. Paul wrote, "Every Sunday each of you must put aside some money, in proportion to what he has earned, and save it up, so that there will be no need to collect money when I come" (I Cor. 16:2). If you give on a regular basis, you give because you are putting God first in your life. If you give once a year, you are doing so to take advantage of the tax laws. It's quite likely that God is not first in your life, and your gift does little to bring about the promises of God in your life.

If you are still worried about whether or not you can make ends meet, meet the needs of others. God blesses us in order to be a blessing. According to Luke 6:38, "Give to others, and God will give to you. Indeed, you will receive a full measure, a generous helping, poured into your hands, all that you can hold". The measure you use for others is the one that God will use for you. There's no way we can out give God.

Remember, there is no better way to get your priorities in order than to "be concerned above everything else with the Kingdom of God and with what he requires of you, and he will provide you with all these other things" (Matt. 6:33). It is an awesome promise from God-our Lord and our Creator. Let's believe Him, and do what He says. The rewards will start immediately and last for all eternity.

God entrusts each of us with certain resources, and He expects us to be good stewards over what we have. A principle emphasized repeatedly in Scripture is that if we do well in using limited resources, we will receive more; but if we misuse what little we have, even that will be taken from us. This is such an important principle that Jesus devoted two of His parables to it: the parables of the pounds (Luke 19:11-26) and of the talents (Matt. 25:14-30).

Two Biblical principles that go together are giving and receiving. If you give, you will receive. Jesus said, "Give, and it shall be given unto you; good measure, pressed down, and shaken together, and running over shall men give into your bosom. For with the same measure that ye mete withal it shall be measured to you again" (Luke 6:38). It's possible to give away and be richer, and it's possible to hold onto things and lose as a result. Scripture says, There is one who scatters, yet increase all the more, and there is one who withholds what is justly due, but it results only in want. The generous man will be prosperous, and he who waters will himself be watered (Prov. 11:24-25, NASB). This is such an important concept. We must be a giving people if ever we are to receive all God wants to give us.

CONCLUSION

If you want your money to take care of you, you have to take care of it. Taking care of your money comes down to two simple rules: (1) Spend what you have left after saving, instead of saving what you have left after spending, and (2) Don't leave your financial future up to fate, chance, or other people. Where money is concerned, nobody plans to fail, they just fail to plan. There's a third fact about money that we all need to understand. It is a fact that needs to be clear if we are to live generously and joyously. Money is a means to an end, not an end unto itself. Money has no innate, built-in worth. In, of, and by itself, money isn't worth didly.

Too many people have looked at money as an end instead of a means. As a result, they never enjoyed the things their money could bring. All they ever did was work to accumulate more of it and then hoarded it when they did. Eventually the wealth they possessed came to possess them. So, "Save money, and money will save you". Here's my most important dictum on dollars-Money is worth only one thing, what you can trade it for. And you should never, not ever, be afraid to trade it for things that make you happy-things that can make your life fuller, richer, sweeter.

Money speaks a language everyone understands. It's a universal provider for most everything but happiness, and a universal passport to most any place but heaven. Spend it accordingly, because you sure can't take it with you. You've never seen a Brink's truck following a hearse. And I'm willing to bet you never will. Finally, if you are truly interested in stopping your hard earned money from running away, here are ten steps to remember:

1. Stop, (and I mean right now) being a compulsive spender.
2. Put some money aside every time you get paid.
3. Change your thinking concerning money.
4. Start declaring that you and money are best friends; best friends never leave one another.
5. Change your environment. If you are only around broke folk or those who spend every dime they make, you will soon be one of them if you're not already.
6. Understand that no one should be more concerned about your future then you are.
7. Get a bank saving and checking account.
8. Be grateful for what you have knowing that there are better days ahead.
9. Don't be afraid to think about money each and every day.
10. Don't forget that old person you saw in chapter four when you closed your eyes.

I pray that you come from under the umbrella of fear and anger, and control your money to keep it from running away from you. Love money and respect it, and it will come to you like a rushing river. Now that we have come to reason together, let us seal our financial success with this prayer:

Lord, we thank you first for being a loving and kind heavenly Father. We ask that You will meet us where we are and that you take us to new heights in You. Work on us in the area of our finances and do a new thing for us. We pray for debt relief for your people and declare more money in our lives-money, not only to live a better life, but money that we will use to be a blessing to others. Now, Lord, as we learn to keep more and spend less, give us the spirit to teach others what we have learned. It is in the name of Jesus the Christ that we pray. Amen!

Works Cited

Boston, Kelvin. Smart Money Moves For African Americans. New York: Berkley Publishing Group, 1996.

Brown, Tony. Empower The People. New York: First Quill Edition, 1998.

Hill, Napoleon. Think And Grow Rich. New York: E.P. Dotton, 1972.

The Holy Bible: The King James Version. Grand Rapids: Zondervan, 2002.

The Holy Bible: The New American Standard Bible. Grand Rapids: Zondervan, 2002.

The Holy Bible: The New Living Translation. Wheaton: Tyndale Publishers, 2004.

Lynch, Peter. Learn To Earn. New York: Fireside Rockefeller Center, 1995.

Murphy, Joseph Dr. The Power of the Subconscious Mind. New York: Bantam Books, 2005.

Tilton, Robert. Dare To Be A Success. Dallas: W.O.F. Publications, 1987.

Trump, Donald. <u>Think Like A Billionaire</u>. New York: Ballantine Book, 2004.

U. S. Census Bureau. 14 May 2006 <http//www.census.gov/>

Watley, William, D. <u>Breaking Financial Barriers</u>. New York: New Seasons Press, 2005.

Wattles, Wallace D. <u>The Science Of Getting Rich</u>. New York: Barnes and Noble, 2007.

www.ingramcontent.com/pod-product-compliance
Lightning Source LLC
Chambersburg PA
CBHW021039180526
45163CB00005B/2200